Here

Poems

First published in 2023 by Annalese Press
134 Towngate
Netherthong
Holmfirth
West Yorkshire HD9 3XZ
England

Copyright © 2002 Toni Thomas

Please Note
All characters and situations appearing
in these pages are in the service of poetry.
Any resemblance to real persons,
living or dead, is purely coincidental.

All rights reserved. No part of this publication
may be reproduced, stored, or transmitted in any
form, or by any means electronic, mechanical or
photocopying, recording or otherwise, without the
express written permission of the publisher.

Cover design and layout by Peter Wadsworth
Fillette à la guirlande de fleurs des champs
by Virginie Demont-Breton

British Library Cataloguing-in-Publication Data
A catalogue record for this book is available on
request from the British Library.

ISBN 978-1-7394457-0-6

Acknowledgements

My appreciation for the publications that featured these poems, albeit in slightly different versions and the contests that appreciated them.

"Judas Tree"   *The Chariton Review*

"All Wool for Her Wheel's Planing"
Bellevue Literary Review

"His Coffee Stained Map of the World"
finalist, *Oberon Prize*, first issue

Book Finalist   *Cleveland State University Poetry Center*

Contents

Part One *Kitchen Fables*

Angel's Rest	3
Baptism	5
Here	6
My Son's Industrious Landscapes	7
Summer Vacation	8
This Marriage	9
Unafraid of Winter	10
For Six Nights	11
Old Wives Tales	12
Girl of the Kitchen Fables	13

Part Two *Shoeless*

Blue Dolls	16
I Remember My Mother	17
Fire Between Our Teeth	19
The Girl Who Never Grew Up	21
His Coffee Stained Map of the World	22
The Moon's Bed	23
The Webbed Fantasies of the Night	24

Part Three *Snowfield*

Callous House	29
String Bean	30
Vagrant	31
It is May	32
Missing	33

You Crack Windows	34
Newport Bay	35
I have One Good Eye	36
Deliverance	37
Indentures	38
This Summer Won't Come Back	39

Part Four *Providence*

The Power of Her Thumbs	43
Now that the Trees Have Stopped Bleeding	44
Abiding	45
In My Back Garden	46
My Children Stumble into School Days	47
Are There Silences	48
The Lover's Initials Pressed	49
Saturday	51
I have Inherited a Tiny House	52
In the Blue Notebook	53
Translucent Wings	54
You Nail Braids of Garlic	55
Is it Possible	56

Come into the garden, Maud,
    For the black bat, night, has flown,
Come into the garden, Maud,
    I am here at the gate alone;
And the woodbine spices are wafted abroad,
    And the musk of the rose is blown.
    For a breeze of morning moves,
    And the planet of Love is on high,
Beginning to faint in the light that she loves
    In a bed of daffodil sky,
To faint in the light of the sun she loves,
    To faint in his light, and to die.

    from *Maud,* Alfred Lord Tennyson

Come into the garden, Maud,
    For the black bat, night, has flown,
Come into the garden, Maud,
    I am here at the gate alone;
And the woodbine spices are wafted abroad,
    And the musk of the rose is blown.
    For a breeze of morning moves,
    And the planet of Love is on high,
Beginning to faint in the light that she loves
    In a bed of daffodil sky,
To faint in the light of the sun she loves,
    To faint in his light, and to die.

    from *Maud*, Alfred Lord Tennyson

PART ONE
Kitchen Fables

Angel's Rest

Yesterday when we made our way slow
fitful up the trail toward Angel's Rest
coaxed our Buddha dog—one hundred pounds
black and panting hard in the heat—
our two children by turns skipping
then slugging their way
anxious for water bottles
for lunch to come with the kettle chips
they covet more than their ham sandwiches
it is easy to forget the promise
of some majestic view at the top
after all, there are so many promises
that count for little in this world.

Sometimes it is hard to keep faith.
We climb up past the stump trees
scorched in the fire of '82
last switchblades
scramble over slick rock toward the summit.
Finally we reach the top
pour our black lab his liter of water
find him a slice of shade
gather our children's hands to behold
what this world can offer—
ample cup of snaking Columbia River
steep gorges, the curved thigh of mountains
we may never reach.

There are small glories in this world
resting spots made of ledge and scree field
days the world snaps open for us

and there is no artist as audacious, as indulgent
as this one.

And I want to say
stop
we can't go back
not for work or money
not for crisp houses, an edged lawn
not to always half wonder
what these stands of Ponderosa pine
the hawkweed, milk vetch, sitka
have prepared for us.

Baptism
—for Ahven

I unpeel orange
pull segments apart to fit
the size of your mouth's nest
careful you untwine the white string
over the spine's tender
savor each bite
drip juice down your neck
loose as a yellow river.

You don't wear the pelted grey sweat suit
you came in anymore
like pretty dresses
want your hair long, no bald spot
want a red wagon
don't say so often *I don't like people.*

When I think of you
it's not cramped for those four years
in the bare room of an orphanage
tending newborns
but of a child who buries her hands
in flower petals, doll's hair, slices of orange
strokes them, guards them
keeps them safe.

Here

You spray the hose in our wade pool
coax stamina
your boat to turn brave
as if god's mercy is fickle.

Your sister practices words in English
cat, dog, house, cookie
eddies along the inner rim of the pool
in her paisley swimsuit.
There is nothing this child won't do
for the love of a family.

Late afternoon.
The yard relieved of the sun's weight.
A past mired in broken barrettes
could almost forget itself
in the lull of this tempered light.

You dig dirt, gather treasure
rusted jacks, a marble with black swirl, hairpin
nest them in your sister's palm.

Here where the blue pool waits
it's hard to believe terrible things can happen
ice flows collapse, seals vanish, forests burn
the world is not just lift
the buoyancy of water.

My Son's Industrious Landscapes

populate the carpet.
He builds with blocks, Legos.
Bridges, watchtowers rise up
get crushed by a metal caterpillar.
His alien spacecraft gobbles cars
miniature trees topple.

He is eight years old
dons jeans, sport sandals
as if they were made for him.
Every disaster on the carpet
subject to ruin, last minute deliverance
depending on the whim of his hand.
No one will have to permanently eat dirt in this game.

My son collects rocks, small bones
amber sand
resurrects words
is too young yet to know
how many covenants with the world
each of us can break.

Summer Vacation

The day tethered to plates of egg, snack time
box lunches, bill paying, swim lessons, training wheels.
Twilight strung down the road's sandbars
like holiday lights in another world.

I bandage wounds, mush up banana
sunblock faces
image poems, sculptures of women
overtaking the path
want to be an alpine lake
skinned with edgy mountains
my waters azure blue
as a sunlit eye.

Is it easy to walk on water
avoid the messy
arrive home arrested by the
day's vivid conversations
ready for meal time, children
dabbling part-time in this other space?

The bug infested wade pool, carpet spills
raised beds of cabbage, carrots, tomato
spaceship pajamas with the split seam
the play dates, thirsty patio pots
jam jars waiting with colored beads.
So many needs call to me
call to me
travel my crowded heart.

This Marriage

of turned soil
bird eaten bean starts
a sun that lifts her head
above the horizon then bleeds

this marriage of salt stained sheets
smoldering flame
wind that whips as it clarifies.

Sometimes I trace your lips
on a chalice
wear white—virginal.
You enter my chamber
naked
your hands burning

and everything seems possible.

Unafraid of Winter

You slingshot the surly knights
demolish the watchtower, moat
dig up the man pummeled with rock
the woman with her back bent
depending on the day
can be a crusader for tiger lilies
pond frogs, the cruise liner of a poet's heart.

Spiders climb your gateway to heaven
a colony of goldfish
our black dog whose seventh life is slipping.

This afternoon you will don purple flippers
a face mask
skim the bottom of the park pool
seek out treasure - a key ring, plastic shark, penny
the days' worth of luck we're told
each shiny thing brings.

For Six Nights

the campsite up the *Sunshine Coast*
glued itself to a slate sky with sleeves streaming.
Not even two blue tarps from the marine store
could hold back the rain.
We pressed beach towels into the tent
mopped up the leak spots.
Amidst the puddles, our damp matted hair
the children's clothes bags soaked through
we set the old copper teapot on the burner stove
boiled water, drank tea
slowly became rain
before another dissolution could claim us.
The fifth day, amidst torrential downpours
we hiked a patchwork of trails
watched reversing falls
ate buns on the deck of a tiny bakery
tucked in the woods.

It is not easy to be summer in August rain
listen to our rubber boots slosh
grow back salt tongued, wet faced and glistening
the oyster shells on the beach already turning
their knobby, pearled emptiness into
the rainwater's white bowls.

On the last day the sky drank blue nectar
we rolled up our sweaters
pulled out shorts, the children's swimsuits
flip flops
took a ferry to the island with sand beaches
water so shallow the sun pools
our bodies turned loose
thankful
reconfiguring the sun as our bride.

Old Wives Tales

They say August is a hag resurrected as lupine
poems are spun out of forgotten grapes
that girls who refuse to marry the day
drink from an empty cup.

See how I attempt to rise up on tiptoe
spoon the moon her supper
sooth your bruises with chickweed, verbena
chamomile
stir bones into the broth

see how I poultice with leaves of comfrey
root of burdock
attempt to settle down the ghosts in your closet
clean jeans, hankies, dress pants
the strict measure of your shirts
offer up to the wind's restitution.

Girl of the Kitchen Fables

You fill my glass with dark juice
dysentery
pronounce ascendency over the yard
line our plants up single file
like the women populating your emails.

In the kitchen jars of stewed tomatoes
applesauce, marionberry jam
measuring cups, many bowls.
How much baking powder
to make a cake rise
help my life keep faith

how many hands to nest this home
these children, this life
without failing
as if virtue is spice cake
never derails
your stockyard of fictions.

PART TWO
Shoeless

Blue Dolls

In the city of my childhood summers were humid
the kind that weld your body to a fire escape.
My mother's damp dress stuck to her thighs
each morning she'd search luck in the neighbor's yard.
When the dark set in we'd swipe the air for lightening bugs
listen to the dusty consolation of her voice singing.
My dad drove truck, went off for two, three days at a time.
Somewhere inside did he dream of the sea?

July brought record heat waves.
We stuck a cheap fan in the living room window
and dad came home crabby, yanked off his tee shirt
with it's half moons under the armpit
grabbed a can of pop, headed for the yard.
Nobody disturbed him for fear he'd snap.

My father can crunch a six pack with his bare hands
says he once saved an eleven year kid from drowning
rescued a dog rope lined to the tailgate of a pickup
had the owner's wise ass words socked away.

In the town I grew up in my father's love was a sword blade
my mother walked tiptoe through our tiny apartment.
If anyone heard complaint it was the wind blistering.

How many crushed cans can make a pyramid
how many days can the girl hide away
with her blue dolls by the yard shed?

I don't ever want to die alone on a smug afternoon in Paris.

I Remember my Mother

her bullets of red enamel
Virginia Slim cigarettes, Venus body
long childcare days
my father always away working till Sunday
when my mother shimmied back into black satin
those elegant dresses salvaged from other days
the ones with curved necklines, a nipped in waist
that inspired men to look her up and down
along the listless aisle of the church pews
made her feel alive again
in a world of strep throat and soiled diapers.

There are holes in the three-family house I grew up in
grape stains that leaked into the carpet
my mother's damp voice inside our lunch boxes
her plastic flamingos aching.
In time nobody sang here.
My mother's canvases, her tubes of paint
dried up in cargo trunks pooled in dust
down the basement.

There are houses with few rooms
houses divided in on themselves
the notion of family insular and hard as a nut.
It is not easy to dream in tight spaces
love motherhood yet know it's not all that contains you
pulverize your most passionate ribbon
till it only comes back to meet you in the twines
of a French knot the funeral director weaves
in your hair.

There are circles of hope I finger
erase in the dust on this table
nights that hold no romance anymore, just weariness

the prospect of raising children alone
in a neighborhood of percale sheets, hedged yards
blue pens, fields of white paper that scratch the dark
empire a secret world beyond bleeding.

Fire Between Our Teeth

It's not that my grandmother's hair swept the floor
it swept her back and sturdy waist
long and silver twined with white till the whole thing
glistened in the afternoon Plymouth sun.
She'd tie it up in a loose knot when it came to
washing the dishes, scrubbing the doctor's floors with that
German diligence that earned her some small compensation.
Once my grandfather passed on in his '50's
squat as a French Canadian tank
she sold the big old house on Cherry Street
her two daughters already married, moved away
took the proceeds, bought a small gingerbread style house
a block from the beach, didn't let herself live there
instead rented the place to a nice family.
Grandma moved into a small place at the front of Nana's
cleaned doctors' offices, chose luscious fabrics
sketched endless drawings specifying the cut, shape
style of the outfits the seamstress, Miss Bertie
would go on to make for her.

I remember that other mysterious life
of fancy boxes filled with veiled straw hats, wool caps
leopard muffs, tartan plaids, mauve berets
depending on what mood swept over her
the boxes and boxes of tissue papered heels
each intended to match a particular coat, dress, skirt set
the part of her that loved mother of pearl hairbrushes
amethyst rings, rhinestone broaches
bus trips to the theater in Boston
that secret life beyond the sensible aprons, ammonia
pot roasts, orthopedic shoes.

It's not that the fire in my grandmother's breast
burnt holes bigger than the homilies of the night could carry
but that it was passed down beyond the daily Mass
into the burnt auburn of my mother's hair

her riding jackets, ball gowns, that fiery insolence
that would make her run off at twenty to Manhattan
then to California with a stuntman
till the family annulled the marriage
brought her back to Flushing to be guarded by the relations.
The fire that let her drown her canvases in ochre
burnt umber, vermillion, in Greenwich Village studio classes
till my dad stepped in —
an orphan from the Bronx in a Lieutenant's uniform
the man who doesn't know how to dance
my mother who is certain she can teach him.
They met in a lower eastside ballroom.
He was about to be shipped off to Bavaria.
She loved lakes, the drama of big mountains, chalets
his Brando looks, a maid to help with the details.

The women in my family have held fire between their teeth.
Some fire goes up in communion wafers, a fox coat
fudge marble ice cream late night
when the world upends and you finally realize
this man you married may never learn to twirl his past
enter your dance floor.
I am the granddaughter who wields blue ink
plies clay into the heavy seductive bodies
of women bent on listening
the one who has fumbled through marriages
spent endless years in school
learning what to be, how to live.
In me a whole world keeps clamoring.

The Girl Who Never Grew Up

likes to dream
drown in May's lack of apology
forget rain smacked roads
a blue Jesus.

With only half a house, two small children
how will she surmount the world
recline in her own garden
contemplate god, death, the ocean
loop time
travel the day in forgotten things?

She will grow up with unruly long hair.
Lead feet.
The chipped shells of so many lost coasts
nailed to her care.

His Coffee Stained Map of the World

The young girl with no socks
has streaked lemon in her hair
wears cut-offs, a midriff shirt that
highlights the curvature of her breasts.
She knows this walkway
takes it beside the fishing boats
the Misty Maiden, Thirsty Scupper
Miss Bertie, Chelsea Rose
gathers small glimpses of
his banded back black hair
ancient nose.

He hauls herring, guts tuna
hoses fish heads off the dock
finishes his shift at four.
Loyally she waits for him on the bench
in front of the tavern
where the dock workers stagger in
weary for their pint of ale.

For two months now he has shown her
his coffee stained map of the world.
She is drunk on his sweat, sweetmeats
the crashing waves of his wider sea.
There is no place his fingers
won't take her to
no place his fingers won't mine.

The Moon's Bed

I remember how my mama's body
sped through summer with a red sail
her bare feet, sundresses punctuated with petals.

But September could turn desperate
the weight of wind, dead leaves
thinned light, our class schedules
overgrown bodies.

Over time the nights closed in.
Flowers turned skeletal.
Her sexy halter tops, trips to the beach
were folded into the ordinary of lunchmeat.

I tried to stay perfect, never sick.
My baby brother came down with croup
and then some
kept mama pacing inside for weeks.

I remember her puffed body
lipstick stained cigarettes
how she would hoist herself up
fevered to find a view.

The Webbed Fantasies of the Night

At one time I thought daydreams held air
were imagination's birthright
could riot a room with wallpaper
pinch the bird to sing
lick stardust
eat with no muzzle.

Now I see they are never just yellow tarts
a perky date
dog that rolls over on your blind spot.

The webbed fantasies of the dark
wear high heels, boot spurs
can gobble words
set up their own voice box
will memorize money then spit
tell you what you can and can't do
leave you on an iced bridge
in a faux fur coat
shoeless, empty.

PART THREE
Snowfield

Callous House

You wear webbed feet
scoff down cake, dinner rolls
pearly rooms
barbecue the vex out of winter

try to disguise his ice field
bench pressed words
no porous.

String Bean

I snap your ends
blanch you in scalding water
explain that in dying now
you will be saved for later.

Is there tragedy in the nature
of postponed beans
bodies tucked into zip lock bags
forced to abstain
like children with prize songs
no place to sing them?

Come winter
verdant green turned spruce forest
you will make your way back
couched in ice
the memory of roses
August's raised bed

will be steamed
set in the glass bowl
your succulence twice blanched
but not completely forgotten.

Only a few of you
will escape down the river
of love's fruited basket
string beans
your long boney legs running as fast
as your lives, words
will carry you.

Vagrant

You shall eat time
before the hours
outmine you.

To sit on a sill all day
counting out
the lost petals of daisy
is no season.

Become wind.

It is May

Look—the irises have let
their purple tongues slit open to sing.
On the steps, weeds inch up
crowd between concrete
ants stagger out of their drowsy
vow faith.

In the constellations my arms dream
the sun is a flushed river
loyal suitor
whatever is lost
still carries seed.

Missing

Chortle of gulls, buried sandal
half nibbled sandwiches
children who let their bare feet
lap water, carry them.

Some don't come back
find it buoyant walking on water
let their potato chips, cake
blue buckets slide away.

Now the sea is penciled
with inner tubes.
They bob up and down
nameless.

On the sand
grownups reach
for binoculars, phones
rehearse death
panic.

You Crack Windows

scoff bread
roof tiles
spear the stars to your trellis.

I watch you whip the yard
into messy
ride hotrod over my plate glass
spill eucalyptus
thirsty kisses once trapped
in my bug jar.

Gone the blue Wedgewood
fry pan, forks and knives.

Come dinnertime
no soup will be fiercer
than the one you are about to
concoct for me.

Newport Bay

Seagulls screech
work boats sidle the quay.
Some say the sea
is a mapmaker's apprentice
shoeless bride.

I wear your necklace
sodden vows
want to drink death down
not just rehearse things

show you
my salvaged pearls
mouth rinsed in seaweed

swim with fish
flash iridescent.

I Have One Eye

to see the world by
navigate trellised words, guardrails, blue jars
as if my life depends on it.
Are some lives conquest and strategy
others a homily to waiting?

People are polite here
mind their own business.
It is easy to forget up the road
at the Lady of Sorrows Church
the Sunday Mass in Spanish
is standing room only.
Faith has many faces.

Outside, my children haul tubes, toys
in and out of the wade pool
squander their bodies in late August light
remind me that perhaps it's not too late
to lip read the dark
to hum, sing again
amid all this beauty
dying.

Deliverance

The maple trees up the left ridge
give off their sap willing into my son's bucket.
He is eight, hauls it to the shed
doesn't know yet about emptiness
blighted roots, love that comes rapt
on a July heat wave, trickles away.
Up the path his sister peels mud off her dance shoes
checks her pink feathers
safeguards the paper cranes she keeps
in an envelope.

At snack time we will lay out a blanket
load ourselves with bread, cheese, pickle
watch the trail of ants make a fuss.
The pots will bubble in the shed
sterilized containers wait on the card table.
The world's winged voices will still
sleep in the drum of my daughter's ear.

Given time, a steady flame
the sap will reduce in the big metal pots.
With help my son will bottle and seal the jars
wager the handsome price he can get.
Our daughter's interest not in money but
the pancakes which this syrup will lathe.

Indentures

I don't want to go out on a day like this
comb through cars, parking lots
grocery stores, sweater factories
while a forgotten girl shines her shoes
in the dust.

How many heads of roses turn wilted petal
or willingly lick their lips
kiss the death wish of the rain?

I'm not saying marry me to the storm
or that lives always get glued back
the left foot a homily to the right
but things need to count for something.

In the orange tongues of poppy
the rain's fickle
the night's traipse with death
the world wants to give herself
back to me.

This Summer Won't Come Back

not the overcrowded lettuce starts
bolted spinach, bush beans
blue wade pool that gulps tubes
noodles, bugs, grassy water.

I could stay up forever
to witness your green tendrils
persistent fingers of ivy.
My children search ditches
pocket mica with the sun's face
a rusted pocketknife, pop cap, spoon.
Diggers of holes, they have no reason
to search for paradise somewhere else.

I sew back buttons, knead bread
want to stop counting the hours
till the hours go missing
want to lounge in the nib of my blue pen
float in an ocean of Shasta daisies.

If paradise is anywhere
surely it must be here, in minute doses
the coneflowers, hemlock, lavender, vetch
risen voices of my children calling
in the ditch where we buried the dead sparrow
our last gold fish, secret notes.

Perhaps one day we will call them back
the dead creatures we once loved
draw their bodies up and into a new season
like Lazarus no longer suffering the grave.
Risen.

PART FOUR
Providence

The Power of Her Thumbs

Here in the street
things fall apart, become
a plague of knife ends
the heart disavows the head
wrists fountain
the man with cancer
begs a miracle
woman in her '80's pleads for
her sister in Washington.

Needles stalk the bed sheets
tray tables, wobble of teacups
like early a.m. in the arms of my mother
years ago when her life
fled toward heaven on jagged glass.

Things get busted
tied up to tubes, monitors.
I can't forget that
the way want can wear a porcelain face
hide a cemetery
anchor to letters with no address.

My grandmother used to gather
pieces of bread plate, broken doll limbs
chipped vases
blue pagodas with their tops missing
spend hours out in her yard shed
crushing their bodies back together
with the power of her thumbs.

Now that the Trees have Stopped Bleeding

the cat prowls the yard
our black lab puts his head in my lap
paws my legs
his brown eyes a show of gravy
loyal friend.

Does anyone know how much I love you
how many maple leaves
I have welded to my bed
the way I court you
inside a blue notebook
stir you into the lentil soup
compost bin
wait patient on the roof
for just a glimpse

seek each day
to die just a little more
so you can live?

Abiding

Nothing seems dark, foreign
irretrievable anymore

even the neighbor down the street
with his crucibles to bear
the slashed job
lovers who walked away
truculent angels

still holds the dream
of a decent life
maybe not razor perfect
but abiding
grass stained
messy
glad for the being here.

In My Back Garden

oriental poppies contemplate light
hold layers of tissue breath
the way our communion dresses did
fold over fold over fold under which
the secret spot beckons.

Come October when the Northwest
truants rain
will anyone remember this garden
the magnitude of the bees' burning
the hollyhock and peonies
rosemary peddling her aromatic scent

will anyone remember
that night I let my hair down
strand upon strand upon strand
and you glided that bamboo comb
till the inlets of my body hummed
then hammered
and there was nothing but hair and
hand upon hand upon hand
in the wide hammock of our christening.

My Children Stumble into School Days

an avalanche of facts
wait on snack time, story hour
recess, colored chalk
the sick bell's homily.

It is September when
some things want to die
flame as fallen leaves
take your breath away
with the spin and strut of their torso.

Come Saturday morning
they slip into bed with me
nuzzle under the blanket
concoct stories.
Their tongues no milky toast
the asps prey on.

I would do almost anything
to postpone the dead lilacs
by their door.

Are There Silences

that count for something
refuse to dine on strict penmanship
plumed words
with their panties bleeding?

You tether to me
accept my muddied taffeta
felt owl on a stick
bird pecks.

The Lovers' Initials Pressed into a Picnic Table Strassel Farm

Nothing moves like your body
through clear air.
The quartz chimes on the porch
spill their voice tingly, a harp playing
as if in seeing you
the world is able to lip read the day.

I imagine four seasons of prosperity
the well behind the pump house full
the black dog not needing to make his way
up the trail on arthritic knees
the apples in the orchard unmaimed
my boy child's missing front tooth
grown back new.

You spend time gathering acorns, chestnuts
ensure nothing gets lost
nail a rope of garlic onto our door
perch by the birdfeeder
till the finch find you.
Even the marsh hawk circling want
above the meadow does not turn away.

Under the ash tree
there sits a table—
marriage of heaven or hell—
depending on the side we enter.
This table has a top of distressed pine.

Four years ago someone carved
our names in the face of it.
The initials won't be weathered away.
Dinked wood from an ancient tree
your honey stained knots lifting.

I sit here. Face you. Face myself.
This picnic worth picnicing.
This life that is burning burning burning
all my black spotted roses away.

Saturday

my life a lapse into the chapel of children
their lemon suns, slippery stars
rabbits and possum
the worn down sheen of their crayons
like certain worn down houses
certain faces
that have not turned the stranger
away from their door.

Stealthy, the moon walks on tiptoe
convinced that maybe silence
can save us.

Your hands are grown of
the silkworm's spinning
cup milky cousins
slide down my thighs
smear streaks of crayon
language my body
with your purple stump
raw into glistening.

I have Inherited a Tiny House

in the trees where the scent of the sea lingers
bought two wicker chairs at a garage sale
to make the porch homey.
Spider sacs tucked in the eaves
ivy making a cemetery of the squash beds.
It looks out on the marshes
blue heron, bent arm of the sun
slips of uncertainty that have spent
a lifetime piling up at my door.

The table under the ash tree
buried in weed, leaf fall.
Deer foraging the orchard
for the last of the roma apples.
One stellar jay above the meadow.

I have inherited a tiny house by the sea.
It has sloped floors, decent shingle
two hanging baskets pressed with geranium.
Their balls spire
confetti the ground
remind me of my mother
her love for me.

Even in the depths of winter
they will hang on.

In My Blue Notebook

I am not half feeble
summit mountains
graze marshland
finger the sea.

Lovers who walked out
of my life
half stay
offer up remnant kisses.

In my blue notebook
each of us gets another chance
to become the reserve of roses
fortune teller's breadbasket

arrive back emptied
grateful.

Translucent Wings

Mud caked fields.
Inside - my daughter's fingers alive
in the tray of strawberries
my son pressing thin lines
onto white paper with his drawing pen.
The beetles with the translucent wings
spread over the patio, picnic table
now that June has proposed to them.

Life beckons
its paper thin wafer
yellow endings.
Look what the breakup of clouds
can do to me.
Everyone notices.
No more runs up my legs
my cotton shift shifting toward heaven.

Indecent
I go around without underwear anymore
legs splayed open.
The only lingering
these lemon wafers
gifts of the sea.

You Nail Braids of Garlic

above my door
find the hand
that saves the hand
smashed in the rain.
I watch you pool the sun
walk away from tank tops
and into your mint dress.

Even the neighbor man who sawed
his mother's prize plum tree
no longer rehearses death
chastens his hands
lets the foxglove forgive him.

Worm, beetle, slug, coyote
yard swing that clutches my children
their kingdoms of sand

in a time of such brokenness
so much psalm.

Is it Possible

everything comes back to us
the calypso orchid
lover with an orphaned face
jeweled layers of onion
dazzle of snowflakes
black dog who echoes the Buddha
begonia, fuchsia willing their way back
and into another spring.

I have seen worn toe shoes
get up and dance
women afraid of their life
reclaim it
the dilapidation of paradise
be drunk down to psalm.

How many summers can railroad
our lives without summering?
In summering fully will I give my life
back to you?

In the house laundry piles up
my children beg mac and cheese
a dinner of tater tots and sausage.
I have seen houses fly away blind
cars lay down to rust
orchids, peonies race past me in bare feet.

I want no more reasons
to hold what is lost
love what remains.
Only this.   This.

Toni Thomas lives in Portland, Oregon. Her poems have been published in Austria, Spain, New Zealand, Canada, England, Scotland, and Australia. In the United States her work has appeared in over fifty literary magazines including *Prairie Schooner, North Dakota Quarterly, Hayden's Ferry Review, the Minnesota Review, Notre Dame Review, Poetry East*, and more. She has been twice nominated for a Pushcart prize, and won several awards. She has published sixteen collections of poetry and four books for children.

Her figurative clay sculptures have been shown in gallery exhibits in Portland and Chicago, displayed in literary magazines, and housed in private collections in the U.S. and England.

Her short documentary *One of Us* was shown at the Trans-ideology: Nostalgia festival in Berlin and at the Museum of
Contemporary Art in Taipei.

Since Toni loves to create and sits buried in reams of poems, manuscripts, clay figures and images….she likes to imagine all of them out in the world swaying wild as the lupine.

tonithomaspoetry.com

www.ingramcontent.com/pod-product-compliance
Lightning Source LLC
Chambersburg PA
CBHW021131080526
44587CB00012B/1242